T·E·R·R·O·R·I·S·M

What Makes a Terrorist?

By Shelley Tougas

Content Adviser: Jarret Brachman, Ph.D., author of *Global Jihadism: Theory and Practice* and senior U.S. government counterterrorism consultant

Reading Adviser: Alexa L. Sandmann, Ed.D., Professor of Literacy, College and Graduate School of Education, Health, and Human Services, Kent State University

COMPASS POINT BOOKS
a capstone imprint

Compass Point Books
151 Good Counsel Drive
P.O. Box 669
Mankato, MN 56002-0669

 Printed in the United States of America in North Mankato, Minnesota.
092009
005618CGS10

Editor: Jennifer Fretland VanVoorst
Designer: Heidi Thompson
Media Researcher: Eric Gohl
Library Consultant: Kathleen Baxter
Production Specialist: Jane Klenk

Image Credits: Alamy/Roger Hutchings, 11; AP Images/Bill Waugh, 4; AP Images/Elaine Thompson, 15; AP Images/Liu Heung Shing, 9; AP Images/Nati Harnik, 21; AP Images/Silvia Izquierdo, 45; Corbis/Bettmann, 31, cover; Getty Images Inc./AFP/Daniel Velez, 37; Getty Images Inc./AFP/Lakruwan Wanniarachchi, 27, 39; Getty Images Inc./AFP/Luis Acosta, 32; Getty Images Inc./AFP/Saeed Khan, 16; Getty Images Inc./AFP/Said Khatib, 28; Getty Images Inc./AFP/Yoshikazu Tsuno, 40; Getty Images Inc./BWP Media/Hugh Thomas, 14; Getty Images Inc./FBI, 25; Getty Images Inc./Natalie Behring, 22; Getty Images Inc./Roland Neveu, 35; Getty Images Inc./Spencer Platt, 43; Newscom, 6.

This book was manufactured with paper containing
at least 10 percent post-consumer waste.

Library of Congress Cataloging-in-Publication Data
Tougas, Shelley.
What makes a terrorist? / by Shelley Tougas.
p. cm.
Includes bibliographical references and index.
ISBN 978-0-7565-4312-9 (library binding)
1. Terrorism—Juvenile literature. 2. Terrorists—Juvenile literature. I. Title.
HV6431.T668 2010
363.325'11—dc22 2009034861

Visit Compass Point Books on the Internet at *www.compasspointbooks.com*
or e-mail your request to *custserv@compasspointbooks.com*

TABLE OF CONTENTS

Two Tales of Terrorism

U.S. Army veteran Timothy McVeigh considered himself a patriot at war. The enemy was his own government.

On April 19, 1995, a sunny spring morning in Oklahoma City, McVeigh parked a truck filled with explosives near the Alfred P. Murrah Federal Building. He lit a fuse and fled in a getaway car. A few moments later, an explosion blew a side off the building. One hundred sixty-eight people were killed. Nearly 700 were hurt.

McVeigh chose to attack on April 19 for an important reason. The date marked the two-year anniversary of the Waco siege. McVeigh wanted revenge against the federal government for the raid.

Thousands of search and rescue workers attended a memorial service in front of the Alfred P. Murrah Federal Building in May 1995.

The Waco siege began when federal agents confronted members of a religious cult near Waco, Texas. The cult leaders were suspected of illegally having weapons. Agents surrounded the property, launching a 51-day standoff. The confrontation ended when the agents fired tear gas into the building. They hoped the tear gas would force those inside to surrender. But it did not. Six hours later, fire swept through the compound, killing 76 members of the Branch Davidian cult.

Although arson investigators said

Timothy McVeigh served in the U.S. Army from 1988 to 1991, earning a Bronze Star for bravery during Operation Desert Storm.

cult members deliberately set the fires, McVeigh thought the federal agents had committed mass murder. The siege confirmed his long-held political beliefs. After spending years studying material that claimed the government abused its power and took rights from citizens, McVeigh was convinced that the claim was true. For him the Oklahoma City bombing was a justifiable act of war.

McVeigh was caught, tried, found guilty, and executed in 2001. He refused to say he was sorry for the bombing. He argued that innocent people die in a war.

Eight years before the bombing in Oklahoma City and thousands of miles away, a North Korean woman named Kim Hyun Hee accepted a mission from her government. The mission's planners told her that she could bring North Korea and South Korea together again if she blew up a plane. The two countries once had been a single country. They separated after World War II and became enemies.

North Korean officials had asked Kim to be a spy when she was just a teenager. During her training, she saw films and writings about the North Korean government. Everything Kim watched and read was propaganda—information, often incomplete or biased, that is used to influence the way people think. She was taught that North Korea had good values. South Korea, however, was shown as a country that had lost its values and hurt its own people.

Leaders picked Kim for the mission partly because she didn't look like a terrorist. Many people expect terrorists to look a certain way. They have a picture of terrorists in their minds from movies and the news. Nobody thought an attractive young woman would deliberately kill innocent people.

Kim and another agent stowed a bomb aboard a South Korean airliner bound for Bangkok, Thailand. She escaped after planting the bomb. The plane exploded in flight over the Indian Ocean, and all 115 people aboard were killed.

South Korean police caught Kim after the explosion. She tried to kill herself to keep the police from learning about her mission, but they stopped her. After her arrest, Kim had a chance to see how South Koreans really lived. It was nothing like what she'd been told. Kim confessed, and she apologized for what she did.

Officials in South Korea pardoned Kim. She was allowed to leave prison and live in South Korea. They said North Korea's leaders were responsible for the bombing because they had planned it.

Timothy McVeigh and Kim Hyun Hee share the label "terrorist" but little else. They were born and raised in very different cultures. The United States is one of the wealthiest nations in the world. North Korea is among the poorest. Citizens of the United States have many freedoms. North Koreans, however, can be jailed or even killed for disagreeing with their government.

McVeigh came from a middle-class family and joined the Army after high school. He earned a Bronze Star, a military medal, for serving the country he would eventually hate. Kim was well-educated. She attended Pyongyang Foreign Language College and Keumsung Military College. Her family had important ties to the North Korean government.

Kim and McVeigh had two things in common. At some point in their lives,

Kim Hyun Hee (right) entered a South Korean court in 1989, where she was sentenced to death. She was pardoned the next year.

both were surrounded by propaganda. They listened only to people who told them to hate an enemy. For McVeigh the enemy was his own country. For Kim the enemy was a neighboring country. And both decided to attack their enemies with violence.

Terrorist Traits

Who are terrorists, and what makes them commit acts of terror? Experts have tried to create a profile of the typical terrorist. A profile is a set of common characteristics. These include age, education, income, and religion. If experts had a reliable profile, they could figure out who is most likely to become a terrorist. Perhaps they could stop people like McVeigh and Kim from carrying out terrible acts.

Do people become terrorists because they are poor and have no other options? Are they mentally ill? Do they lack an education? Are they religious? Or do they reject religion? Making a good profile has proved impossible. Terrorists' characteristics vary, just as other people's do.

Experts who study terrorism have found only a few common traits. The traits are so general, however, that they do not make a complete profile. It's also important to note that although certain causes tend to be associated with certain kinds of terrorists, there are many exceptions. Here are some traits experts have found in many terrorists:

- Terrorists tend to be young. Terrorist training involves hard physical activity, much like the military. Members must be strong to carry and use heavy weapons. Terrorist leaders, however, tend to be older. Their age and experience help them make decisions and train new members.
- Terrorists are usually unmarried. Terrorists have to move around and use fake identities. They go someplace for training and then

The Liberation Tigers of Tamil Eelam, also known as the Tamil Tigers, is a terrorist group that recruits young people.

disappear for missions. Family responsibilities make it difficult to carry out the work of a terrorist.

- Terrorists are mostly men. There are many exceptions, particularly in certain countries. In Germany, for example, a woman named Ulrike Meinhof was the founder of a terrorist group called the Red Army Faction. (The group was also called the Baader-Meinhof Gang.) In Sri Lanka, thousands of children and women belong to the Liberation Tigers of Tamil Eelam—a terrorist group better known as the Tamil Tigers.

Terrorists hold extreme views, of course, but beliefs alone do not make a terrorist. Many people hold extreme views. Some people with strong opinions run for political office. They write letters to newspapers, call radio talk shows, or organize protests. They try to influence leaders and citizens to support their cause. They may say things that don't make sense to other people or make other people angry. But they don't turn to violence.

Terrorists are either unable or unwilling to change the world in acceptable, nonviolent ways. They use fear and violence against people to achieve a goal. Terrorists believe their goals are more important than life.

But terrorists don't see themselves as evil. In fact terrorists think they are the solution to an urgent problem. They believe they are making great sacrifices for an important cause. Terrorists believe they are at war, but they are fighting a different kind of war. In most cases, they don't have a traditional military force, with uniforms, weapons, and bases. They usually don't have the support of a country's government. And while they may target the military, terrorists also try to hurt and scare ordinary people.

It may sound as if terrorists are mentally unstable. Why would they leave their

How Much Alike Are Well-Known Terrorists?

Experts have tried to learn what terrorists have in common, such as age, education, income, and religion. With such a profile, they could better figure out who might become a terrorist. Here is what some well-known terrorists do—and don't—have in common.

Terrorist	Religion	Terrorist Group	Educational Level	Criminal Acts	Quick Facts
Timothy McVeigh (United States)	Catholic	None	High school	Oklahoma City bombing	Left military feeling angry about the U.S. government; held low-skill jobs
Osama bin Laden (Saudi Arabia)	Islam	al-Qaida	University	Masterminded September 11 attacks and many others	Raised in a large, wealthy family; attended elite schools
Ulrike Meinhof (Germany)	Born to a Protesant family, but did not practice religion	Red Army Faction / Baader-Meinhof Gang	University	Bombing government buildings, bank robberies, prison escape	Wanted social justice; thought the government was oppressive; killed herself in prison
Theodore Kaczynski (United States)	Atheist	None	University; graduate school	Several mail bombings; became known as the Unabomber	Lived alone in the wilderness; his brother led authorities to arrest him
Kim Hyun Hee (North Korea)	Atheist; later became a Christian	Worked for the North Korean government	University; special training to be a secret agent	Blew up a South Korean airliner	Confessed her crime and was pardoned by South Korea

homes and travel secretly across the world? Why would they pretend to be someone they are not? Why would they deliberately hurt or kill people and destroy property? But most terrorists do not seem to have a mental illness. They have simply devoted themselves to a cause. They have stopped listening to opinions different from their own and are willing to commit violent acts to achieve their goals.

Leaders of terrorist groups generally avoid recruiting members with mental problems. Terrorists need to be calm in stressful events. They must follow orders and not make mistakes. Leaders need members who can act and look like ordinary people. That's how terrorists are able to blend into society and carry out their missions. If terrorists acted strangely, they would call attention to themselves. The police might learn about their plans and stop them.

Parents comforted their children after a September 2001 bombing in Belfast, Northern Ireland.

After the Oklahoma City bombing, a psychiatrist talked to McVeigh in prison. The psychiatrist said McVeigh was not delusional, which is a sign of mental illness. But McVeigh had let his anger grow out of control. He expressed his rage in one violent, murderous event.

Are Terrorists Mentally Ill?

You'd have to have suffered a break from reality to set off a bomb in a store or fly a plane into a building when you know you will die, right? Wrong. People who study terrorists have learned that they are not mentally ill. Terrorists have become so devoted to their cause that they are willing to hurt or kill people. Some terrorists are willing to kill themselves. They don't consider their actions monstrous or evil. They believe they are freedom fighters.

Theodore Kaczynski

Of course, there are exceptions. One of America's most famous terrorists is Theodore Kaczynski. Once a promising young scientist, he was diagnosed with a mental illness called paranoid schizophrenia. Kaczynski left his job and built a cabin in the wilderness. He lived alone, without electricity or running water. He wanted to start a revolution against technology.

Over the course of two decades, he sent bombs in the mail. Three people were killed, and 16 were injured. The news media began calling him the Unabomber. When he was finally arrested, a psychiatrist diagnosed his illness. Kaczynski was sentenced to life in prison.

JEHAD
IS HOLY
WAR AGAINST
1999

Terrorism and Religion

You may have read or seen news stories about terrorism and religion. Religious beliefs do seem to lead many terrorists to commit violent acts.

Americans have been focused on Islamic terrorists since September 11, 2001. On that day, a group of Islamic terrorists attacked the United States. Terrorists flew two airliners into the World Trade Center in New York City. The buildings collapsed, killing thousands of people. A third airliner crashed into the Pentagon, the headquarters of the U.S. Department of Defense. Terrorists see the Pentagon as a symbol of the U.S.

Followers of the Islamic terrorist group al-Qaida called for a holy war against the United States.

military. On another plane, passengers fought back against the terrorists. The passengers stopped the plane from reaching the White House or the U.S. Capitol, which apparently were other targets of the terrorists. The plane crashed into a field near Shanksville, Pennsylvania, killing everyone on board.

The September 11 attacks were organized by al-Qaida, a terrorist group that wants to end foreign involvement in Muslim nations. The group supports a very strict form of the Islamic religion, one that most Muslims believe to be un-Islamic. Al-Qaida also has been responsible for many attacks against the American military in Iraq. The citizens of Iraq are often victims, too.

To al-Qaida members, Islam allows them to kill people—including themselves—in a holy war. (Although suicide is forbidden in Islam, al-Qaida members believe that dying in order to kill others is not suicide.) The Islamic name for the holy war is *jihad*, which means "to struggle" in Arabic. Al-Qaida members believe that the main struggle for Muslims is violent and is against anyone who disagrees with their interpretation of Islam—even other Muslims. Al-Qaida terrorists believe they are saving their fellow citizens from a far greater evil. They think the United States is destroying their way of life and stealing their countries' wealth.

It's important to note that most people of the Islamic faith oppose al-Qaida and oppose violence. They don't think the Islamic holy book, the Qur'an, calls for or supports terrorists' acts of violence. Most Muslims believe that terrorists have twisted their religion in an evil way.

Suicide Attackers

Some terrorist groups use suicide attackers, also called suicide bombers, to carry out assaults. Suicide attackers know they will die during their missions. But they believe so deeply in their cause that they are willing to die for it.

Suicide attackers are usually associated with Islamic terrorists in the Middle East and the Liberation Tigers of Tamil Eelam in Sri Lanka.

Many suicide attackers believe they will receive great rewards in heaven. Sometimes their families receive money as a reward. In some countries, the pictures of suicide attackers are put on posters or cards to celebrate their sacrifices. Suicide attackers are turned into heroes.

Suicide attacks give terrorists several advantages. There is no need to plan an escape. Their missions don't need to be complicated or costly. Bombs don't have to be delivered by a missile or remote control. It is easy for an average-looking person to walk into a busy market, subway, or other public place and not create any suspicion.

Terrorist leaders give suicide attackers special training so they look normal and act normally. The trainers also make sure suicide attackers don't have second thoughts or change their minds. They help them deal with feelings of fear. They make sure they can't remove their bombs at the last minute.

Some terrorist leaders have tricked people with mental illnesses into becoming suicide attackers. But most suicide attackers volunteer for the job. They are willing to die for their cause.

Many people of faith care deeply about their religion. Most religious people believe it's wrong to hurt or kill people. But there are terrorists who claim they are carrying out God's will. They believe God is on their side. They say their victims are enemies of God. These terrorists expect special rewards in heaven because they're fighting a war for God.

Terrorism doesn't have a home with any single religion. Christians have bombed abortion clinics across the United States. A religious cult called Aum Shinrikyo released poison gas into the subway system in Tokyo. A Jewish doctor, Baruch Goldstein, killed a group of Muslims praying in the Palestinian city of Hebron.

Many experts who study terrorism say religion is often a mask for politics. In some countries, citizens are not allowed to speak about politics. They don't have the freedom to question their own governments. In these countries, religion is a part of life that allows expression and active involvement. To the outside world, it seems that terrorism is driven simply by religion. A closer look, however, shows that religion and political beliefs are often tied together.

Not all terrorists are religious. Some terrorists claim no religion at all. Many terrorists want to rid the world of religion. Some terrorist groups have taken on nonreligious causes. They fight for animal rights or to save the environment, for example. For much of the 20th century, several terrorist groups tried to spread communism. Communism is a form of government in which the government controls a country's wealth.

Firefighters and arson investigators worked to determine the cause of a January 2009 fire at a Nebraska abortion clinic.

97

Education and Income

Religion is just one factor studied by terrorism experts. They want to know as much as possible about the lives of terrorists. So they also are interested in terrorists' education and income.

Some countries have few schools because they are so poor. It's not surprising that terrorists from these countries have little education. Some terrorist groups are run like a low-tech military. Their members don't need to be well-educated. They only need to know how to use weapons and follow orders. They are basically bodies for combat. The leaders teach recruits everything they need to know.

Terrorist groups need members with skills and education, so they often try to recruit university-educated young people.

Wanted: Terrorist

If a terrorist leader were taking out a job ad in a newspaper, it might read something like this:

> Seeking well-educated people who speak several languages. Must have skills in computers, engineering, science, and communications. Must be able to act comfortably in foreign countries. Must be able to carry out complex tasks and live a secret life. Travel required.

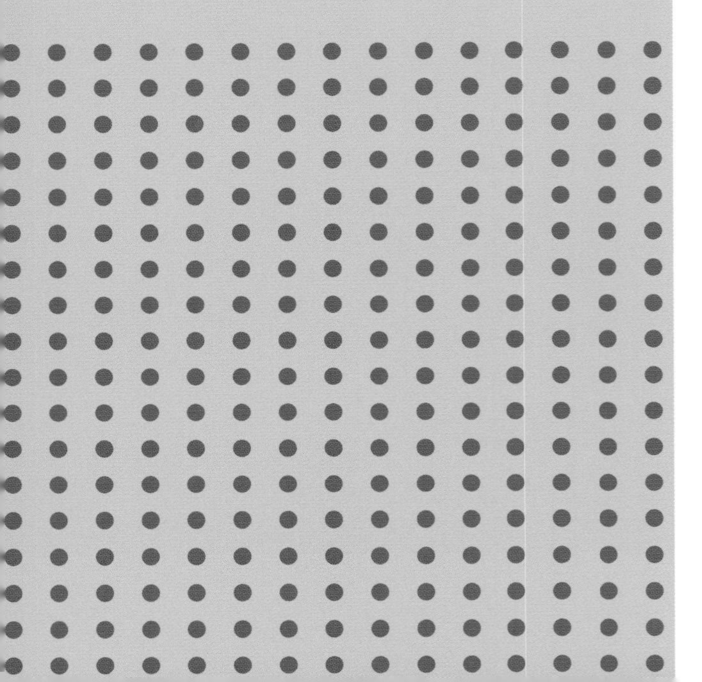

But this doesn't tell the whole story. Many terrorist organizations have little use for people without skills and education. It takes brainpower to plan and carry out an attack. Mistakes could tip off police and ruin years of planning.

Researchers have found that many terrorists have college educations. Many come from middle-class families. In Germany two terrorist groups recruited only from a university. Those groups were known as the June Second Movement and the Baader-Meinhof Gang.

After the September 11 attacks, the U.S. government formed a commission to study what happened. The commission found that many of the hijackers were recruited at colleges. Most were from middle-class families. In fact al-Qaida's leader, Osama bin Laden, is from a wealthy family and received a university education.

For decades many researchers believed poverty was the main cause of terrorism. If you were poor, they thought, you were more likely to become a terrorist.

A connection between poverty and terrorism makes sense. Young people without jobs seem to be easy recruits because they have few options. They are bored, restless, and often angry. They may believe their poverty and other problems were caused by a certain leader or another country. If they have never felt valued, a leader can make them feel important.

But researchers no longer believe that people become terrorists simply because they're poor.

Most of the hijackers in the September 11 attacks were well-educated, and many were recruited at colleges.

Some researchers have studied the links among terrorism, money, and education. They've looked at surveys of rich people and poor people in countries with high rates of terrorism. The surveys show that people with money are more likely than poor people to take part in terrorist acts.

Political involvement requires interest, knowledge, and time. People living in poverty spend almost all their time working to survive and feed their families. They don't have the opportunity to learn much about government, history, and economics in school. They can't afford books. They don't have money to travel and learn about the world.

Terrorist leaders also need wealthy people to support their causes. They need money to buy weapons and bombs. It's expensive to travel and train. Terrorist leaders need people who understand finance and accounting so they can hide money. Otherwise police could track what terrorists were buying and figure out their plans. Some terrorist groups commit crimes, such as stealing or selling drugs, to get money for their missions.

Some exceptions are terrorist groups that operate like a military organization. Examples include the Revolutionary Armed Forces of Colombia (FARC), the Liberation Tigers of Tamil Eelam (Tamil Tigers) in Sri Lanka, and the Irish Republican Army (IRA) in Northern Ireland. Most of these groups' members come from working-class families.

Children as Terrorists

In Sri Lanka a terrorist group Liberation Tigers of Tamil Eelam has a special unit made up entirely of children. In some parts of the country, children are forced to join the group and fight. Children serve in every type of position except for leadership roles.

There are no age limits to be a terrorist. Most terrorists are adults, but terrorist leaders use children when it helps their cause. Police don't think children will be carrying bombs and guns. Terrorist leaders use children to fool police and the public.

In some communities, suicide attackers are considered heroes. Their faces are on posters, which are displayed in public places. Their sacrifices are celebrated. Suicide attackers are admired in the same way many children admire athletes, rock stars, and actors. Children in any country want to follow in the footsteps of their heroes.

Terrorist leaders find it easy to persuade children to join their cause. Children do not have much experience. They count on adults to help them understand the world. In some cases, children are even forced to fight. They might agree to go on suicide missions without fully understanding what will happen to them.

القسام

Political Rights

If some terrorists aren't driven to terrorism by a lack of money or education, or by their religion, then what does drive them? Many researchers believe there is a connection between terrorism and a lack of political rights.

In countries where citizens have political rights, people can vote in elections without fear. They can express their opinions in public and write letters to the newspaper. They can run for office and tell lawmakers what changes they want in law. They aren't afraid the police will arrest them for saying what they think. These political rights belong to everyone. Skin color doesn't matter, nor does religion, or whether a person is a man or woman.

Palestinians exercised their political rights by protesting an Israeli blockade in 2009.

Countries without these rights tend to have more terrorism. That's because terrorist activities are seen as the only way to change the world. In these countries, people go to prison for criticizing the government. You can only be part of the government if you're born into the right family or if you have the right friends. Voting is difficult or impossible, and violence may be common. People begin to see violence as a normal part of life.

Countries with political rights can also produce terrorists, of course. Timothy McVeigh, who bombed the federal building in Oklahoma City, was raised in the United States. The United States has an open government and a history of political rights. Still McVeigh chose to kill people instead of working for change in nonviolent ways.

The Symbionese Liberation Army also operated in the United States. During the 1970s, this group robbed banks, kidnapped wealthy newspaper heiress Patty Hearst, and killed a California school superintendent and a bank customer. They viewed the United States as a corrupt, racist society.

Why would educated, middle-class people from countries with political rights turn to terrorism? It's often because they feel deep guilt about the world's problems. They feel bad that they have money and are educated and in good health while other people suffer. Many turn to extreme ideas. They believe they can help the poor and oppressed through violence.

In addition to studying ideas about religion, education, money, and political rights, experts have wondered about the process of becoming a terrorist. How does someone leave his or her normal life behind and turn to terrorism? It can't be easy for people to leave their families. It must be difficult to plan the deaths of other people and to think

The Symbionese Liberation Army distributed a publicity photo of Patty Hearst after she joined her captors' cause.

about dying, even for a worthy cause.

The experts who study this question are psychologists and sociologists rather than political scientists, historians, or economists. These experts study how people think and act when they are alone and when they are in groups. Some researchers think it's more important to learn about how terrorists connect with each other than to create a profile. They think terrorist groups are similar to religious cults. In both kinds of groups, members slowly lose their identities. The group absorbs the individual.

Military-style dress helps reinforce a sense of group identification among members of the Revolutionary Armed Forces of Colombia.

Women as Terrorists

In 1991 a woman approached former Indian Prime Minister Rajiv Gandhi. She pretended to be a well-wisher so she could get close to him. Then she set off a bomb hidden under her clothes. Gandhi, the woman, and more than a dozen others were killed.

Women are valuable members of terrorist groups. Police and the public don't expect them to carry weapons. They don't expect women to hurt or kill people. A man might not have been able to get as close to Gandhi as the female terrorist did.

Women are a minority of terrorists in most countries, but not all. The 1970s were years of great social and political trouble in some countries, including the United States. During that time, women were involved in terrorism. A group known as the Symbionese Liberation Army had active female members in the United States. In Germany a terrorist group called Red Zora recruited only women. Two other well-known German terrorist groups also relied on women. The groups had more women as members than men.

The group responsible for killing Gandhi is the Liberation Tigers of Tamil Eelam. This group recruits women to join its forces and fight. Some women are recruited to terrorist groups by men they love. Others join because they believe in the cause. The group uses women as suicide attackers. Leaders tell women that dying for the cause is the only way to show they are as brave as men.

A Sense of Belonging

Human beings have a deep need to belong to a group. A group may be a family, friends, a church, or a club. Terrorist leaders use this basic human need to their advantage.

When people join a terrorist group, they believe they are part of something important. They are suddenly part of something bigger than themselves. Many young men crave adventure, and fighting for a cause fills their need for adventure and glory. This is especially true when they are fighting with close friends. They feel like part of a special family that has an important cause.

Sometimes new members don't need to be recruited. People might seek out the organization because they want to join. They don't have to be convinced that the group's cause is right. They already support the cause.

Certainly some terrorists operate

Young members of the Palestinian Liberation Organization in front of a poster of their leader, Yasir Arafat, in 1983

alone, or with a partner. Theodore Kaczynski, known as the Unabomber, worked alone. Only one other person, Terry Nichols, was convicted of helping Timothy McVeigh blow up the federal building. He is serving a life sentence in prison.

But people who join terrorist groups don't just sign up, get a gun, and start planning attacks. The process takes time. Former members of terrorist organizations have told stories about how they came to be involved in terrorist activities. Based on their collective experiences, here's one example of how a person might turn to terror:

You are a teenage boy growing up in a country with a history of conflict. Your country doesn't have many political freedoms. Many of your neighbors are poor, but your family has more money than most. Your father owns a large store. Your mother has raised you and your brothers and sisters.

Members of a radical group are always in the news. The newspapers call them terrorists. Some people think they're heroes. The group's leaders say they're trying to stop other nations from ruining your country. The other nations, the terrorists say, have caused fighting and poverty. They've taken your country's resources, and your own government has allowed it to happen.

When you look around, you see suffering. You see children who can't go to school because they work to support their families. Your father tells you about customers who can't afford to pay him. He often gives customers what they need in exchange for things such as eggs or milk instead of money. Your government seems more interested in pleasing powerful countries than helping its own people.

Although you don't like what the terrorists do, you believe in their cause. You believe that they are fighting against unfairness. They are fighting to stop the bad influences in your country. The group is giving a voice to people without a voice.

When you go to the university, you meet many young people with families like yours. You share their opinions and beliefs. You stay up late at night discussing politics and debating world events. You are deeply frustrated because things

A French newspaper announced a cease-fire by the terrorist group ETA.

aren't changing. In fact they seem to be getting worse.

Your grades could be better. You don't spend enough time studying. Instead you play soccer with your friends and talk about politics at home. You also spend a lot of time online. You aren't searching to learn more about people who disagree with you. You're visiting chat rooms and Web sites that support your views.

Then you hear terrible news. Government officers have shot people in your hometown when they protested. A former neighbor was killed. Several people, including your uncle, were arrested. You are angry, but you feel helpless. You and your friends discuss the situation day and night.

A friend from the university introduces you to an older man. The man tells you he knows people who are fighting evil in your country. He invites you to join his group. You believe this may be the only way to help your friends and neighbors. You think this group will allow you to make a difference in the world.

This scenario shows how an ordinary person might enter the world of terrorism. Once a person joins a group of terrorists, he or she becomes cut off from the rest of the world. Terrorist leaders don't want members to hear other opinions. New recruits must be surrounded by the opinions and beliefs of the group's members.

A member of the Tamil Tigers gave instructions to new recruits in the Sri Lankan village of Uthayanagar East in 2006.

Of One Mind

As in a religious cult, members of a terrorist group must think and act the same. There is no room for disagreement. The leaders are in control. They make sure new members see the world as "us" against "them." The world is black and white, with no shades of gray.

In normal life, people are influenced by various groups. A family may have one set of opinions. The opinions may be different from the opinions of other families or of friends. And their opinions may be different from those held by church members. Teachers may have still different opinions.

A member of the religious cult Aum Shinrikyo wore headgear that members were told would transmit their leader's brainwaves to them.

In a terrorist group, however, a variety of opinions doesn't exist. There is only one opinion. Group members spend every day repeating that one single opinion. This process is called groupthink. It bonds the members of the group together. They become like family members who will die for each other and their cause. Groupthink is extremely powerful.

New members may be sent away for training, where they learn to use weapons and build up their strength. They learn to think differently about the people they will target. They call their victims "pigs" or "Satan" or other names. If they feel their victims are less than human, or evil, it becomes easier to hurt or kill them.

Members with special skills may take on certain jobs. People with an education may be needed to set up a computer network, build bombs,

Signs of Groupthink

Groupthink is a word popularized by social psychologist Irving Janis. It describes how groups can fall into a pattern of bad decision-making. Experts believe groupthink occurs among members of terrorist groups. There are eight characteristics of groupthink:

1. Members firmly believe they will succeed. This can lead to taking extreme risks.
2. Members ignore other ideas and warnings. They never question what they're thinking.
3. Members believe deeply in their cause. They don't think about the consequences of their actions.
4. Members share a negative view of their enemy.
5. Members are pressured not to argue against the group's views.
6. Members do not express their doubts or concerns.
7. Members assume that everyone in the group agrees.
8. Members protect the group and leader from any information that does not support the group's views and decisions.

The Ku Klux Klan promotes a white-controlled society in the United States by terrorizing members of minority groups, especially blacks.

or create secret bank accounts for the group's money. Everyone has a role. Some members may be chosen to die for the cause. This is considered to be a special sacrifice, and those who willingly die become heroes.

In larger terrorist groups, members are often separated into smaller groups called cells. Members of different cells know very little about each other. This secrecy protects the larger group. If police break up one cell and question its members, they won't learn much, because the members don't know anything about the other cells. The terrorists can continue their fight.

Researching the backgrounds of terrorists has been difficult. The influences of religion, education, poverty, and politics are not easy to sort out. But it has been clearly shown that terrorists are not mentally ill. Terrorists don't believe they are committing evil acts. In fact they think they are fighting evil and making the world a better place.

Terrorists are willing to kill people to promote their ideas. Some of them will give up their own lives for the cause. But before they pick up weapons, they need to form a bond with their group. They come together and learn to think the same thoughts and share the same beliefs. Members of the group care deeply about living the same way of life.

The group connections may offer insight into fighting terrorism. To stop terrorism, the links in the chain of terrorism need to be broken. The links include young people with strong ideals from regions with conflict. Another link is a lack of political freedom. The groupthink that bonds members together is yet another link.

A group with a cause can turn a sensible, ordinary person into a terrorist. Creating terrorists is easier if young recruits are filled with restless energy and anger against people in power. The terrorist group fulfills the need for adventure and brotherhood.

Terrorism doesn't have a home in one country or with one religion or race. Unfortunately terrorism belongs to the entire world. If we want to stop terrorism today and prevent it tomorrow, we must continue to study and learn from the stories of people who have carried out acts of terror.

Children in Lima, Peru, held signs calling for peace at a vigil for victims of the Shining Path terrorist group.

Glossary

atheist—person who believes there is no God

cells—subgroups of a larger organization

communism—political system in which goods and property are owned by the government and shared in common; communist rulers limit personal freedoms to achieve thier goals

corrupt—characterized by improper conduct

cult—small group of people devoted to a person, idea, object, movement, or work

delusional—strongly holding onto false beliefs in spite of evidence proving them incorrect

groupthink—pattern of thought characterized by self-deception and conformity to group values

hijackers—terrorists who forcefully take control of a vehicle, usually an airplane

Islamic—relating to Islam, a religion founded on the Arabian Peninsula in the seventh century by the prophet Muhammad; believers say he was the last human to speak for God, and that his teachings must be followed; believers are know as Muslims

jihad—holy war waged on behalf of Islam as a religious duty

profile—biographical sketch

propaganda—information used to influence the thinking of people; often not completely true or fair

siege—surrounding of a place in order to cut off supplies and force the surrender of those inside

terrorist—person who uses violence and destructive acts to create fear and to achieve a political or religious goal

Additional Resources

Further Reading

Espejo, Roman, ed. *What Motivates Suicide Bombers?* Detroit: Greenhaven Press, 2009.

Gupta, Dipak K. *Who Are the Terrorists?* New York: Chelsea House, 2006.

Landau, Elaine. *Suicide Bombers: Foot Soldiers of the Terrorist Movement.* Minneapolis: Twenty-First Century Books, 2007.

Levin, Jack. *Domestic Terrorism.* New York: Chelsea House, 2006.

Yancey, Diane. *The Unabomber.* Detroit: Lucent Books, 2007.

Internet Sites

FactHound offers a safe, fun way to find Internet sites related to this book. All of the sites on FactHound have been researched by our staff.

Here's all you do:
Visit *www.facthound.com*
FactHound will fetch the best sites for you!

Look for other books in this series:

Combating Terrorism
The History of Terrorism
Terrorist Groups

Select Bibliography

Cigler, Allan J. *Perspectives on Terrorism.* Boston: Houghton Mifflin, 2002.

Cragin, R. Kim, and Sara A. Daly. *Women as Terrorists: Mothers, Recruiters, and Martyrs.* Santa Barbara, Calif.: Praeger Security International, 2009.

Halliday, Fred. *Two Hours That Shook the World: September 11, 2001: Causes and Consequences.* London: Saqi, 2002.

Hudson, Rex A. *Sociology and Psychology of Terrorism.* Hauppauge, N.Y.: Nova Science Publishers, 2009.

Kim, Hyun Hee. *The Tears of My Soul.* New York: William Morrow & Co., 1993.

Krueger, Alan B. *What Makes a Terrorist: Economics and the Roots of Terrorism.* Princeton, N.J.: Princeton University Press, 2007.

Moghaddam, Fathali M. "The Staircase to Terrorism: A Psychological Exploration." *American Psychologist.* February–March 2005.

Stern, Jessica. *The Ultimate Terrorists.* Cambridge, Mass.: Harvard University Press, 1999.

Turchie, Terry D., and Kathleen M. Puckett. *Hunting the American Terrorist: The FBI's War on Homegrown Terror.* Palisades, N.Y.: History Pub. Co., 2007.

Index

About the Author

Shelley Tougas is a former journalist who enjoys following politics and events in the news. Tougas lives with her family in North Mankato, Minnesota. When she's not writing books and articles, she likes reading stories for both children and adults.